KU-632-972

Experiments with

LIGHT AND SOUND

TREVOR COOK

W
FRANKLIN WATTS
LONDON•SYDNEY

First published in 2009 by Franklin Watts

Copyright © 2009 Arcturus Publishing Limited

Franklin Watts
338 Euston Road
London NW1 3BH

Franklin Watts Australia
Level 17/207 Kent Street, Sydney, NSW 2000

Produced by Arcturus Publishing Limited,
26/27 Bickels Yard, 151–153 Bermondsey Street,
London SE1 3HA

ELIN	
Z777940	
PETERS	11-Jul-2012
534	£12.99

The right of Trevor Cook to be identified as the author
of this work has been asserted by him in accordance
with the Copyright, Designs and Patents Act 1988.

All rights reserved.

Editor: Alex Woolf
Designers: Sally Henry and Trevor Cook
Consultant: Keith Clayson
Picture Credits: Sally Henry and Trevor Cook

Every attempt has been made to clear copyright.
Should there be any inadvertent omission,
please apply to the publisher for rectification.

A CIP catalogue record for this book is available
from the British Library.

Dewey Decimal Classification Number: 534

ISBN 978 0 7496 8352 8

Printed in China

Franklin Watts is a division of Hachette Children's Books,
an Hachette Livre UK company.
www.hachettelivre.co.uk

Contents

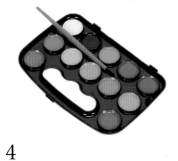

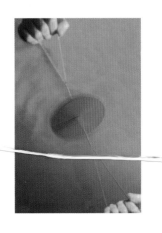

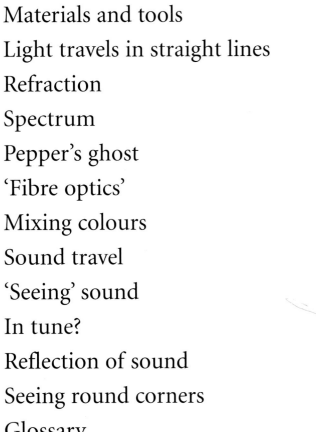

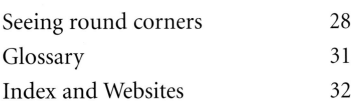

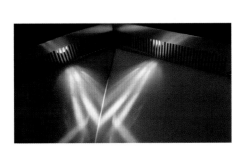

Introduction

The main source of energy we have on the Earth comes to us as heat and light, across the near-vacuum of space from our nearest star, the Sun. Light is *essential* to life on Earth, and not just for us to see our way.

Green plants must have light energy to *convert* minerals into the chemicals they need to grow.

Many tools that use light, such as lenses and mirrors, interfere with its path and seem to bend it and make it change direction. They all work because light is very *precise* and *predictable*. Without interference, the way it travels is about the straightest line there is.

We'll look at *lenses* and mirrors on pages 9–15.

Ancient fortune-tellers used mirrors to make strange images appear in smoke. You can make your own *illusion* on page 14.

A long time ago, a scientist and mathematician called Sir Isaac Newton showed that sunlight could be divided into separate colours, always the same ones, which couldn't be split any further. Try a simple way of seeing the visible spectrum on page 12. You can try different ways of mixing colours back together on pages 13 and 19.

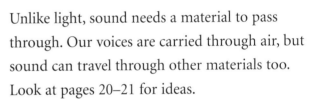

Unlike light, sound needs a material to pass through. Our voices are carried through air, but sound can travel through other materials too. Look at pages 20–21 for ideas.

A foghorn is a warning for ships at sea when it's too foggy to see properly. Experience proves that lower notes work best, but it's still hard to know what direction a sound is coming from.
See what happens when you try to hear round corners on page 26.

Some technical or unusual words, shown in *italic* type, are explained in the glossary on page 31.

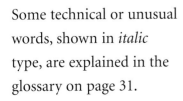

5

Materials and tools

You should easily find many things that you need for our experiments around the home.

20 minutes This tells you about how long a project could take.

 This symbol means you might need adult help.

Tape We use sticky tape to hold things in position. A tape dispenser makes it easier to tear off small pieces.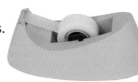

Parcel tape When we need to make stronger joins it's best to use wider, brown tape which is good for sticking cardboard.

Glue stick Mostly used for sticking paper to paper. Universal glue is a rubbery stuff that sticks most things to most other things!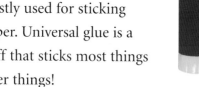

Tubes Collect cardboard tubes from kitchen towels or other paper rolls to use in experiments (see pages 26–27).

Food dye Small bottles of food dyes are available from supermarkets.

Transparent **coloured plastic** Sometimes called 'acetate' – found in craft shops or in music shops, the sheets are often used for disco lighting.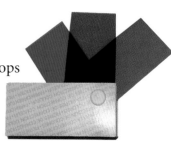

Scissors Ask an adult for an old pair of scissors that you can keep for all your experiments – they will be very useful. Keep them away from young children.

Plastic dropper Available from art and craft shops, ideal for controlling drops of liquid.

String Ordinary household string will be fine for most of our needs.

Plastic bottles Ask an adult for empty plastic bottles. The ones used for water and soft drinks are best.

Shoe box Every time someone has new shoes, there might be be a box available for you.

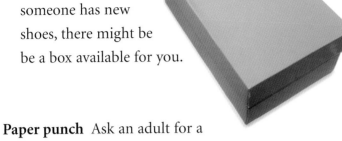

Notebook Keep a special notebook to record the results of your experiments.

Paper punch Ask an adult for a machine so you can cut perfect circles in thin card.

Torch Look out for a small battery-powered flashlight which you will need for Fibre Optics and Mixing Colours.

Plastic mirrors Available from art and craft shops or plastics dealers. Ideal and safe, plastic mirrors can be scored and snapped to size quite easily.

Matches Always take great care with matches. Ask an adult to help you. Don't leave matches lying about.

Paints and brushes Poster paint or ready-mixed colours are ideal for your experiments.

Balloon You will need a balloon on page 23.

Coloured markers You will find it handy to have a box of coloured pens for several of the projects.

Friends can help! Do the experiments with your friends when you can, especially the one on page 30.

Light travels in straight lines

Light is a form of energy that can travel from one place to another.

35 minutes

The plan

We are going to show that light travels in straight lines but we can change its direction.

You will need:

- black card, hole punch
- several different combs
- sticky tape, torches, matchbox
- big sheet of white paper
- small plastic mirror

Experiment 1

hole in card

1 Punch a hole in the piece of card.

2 Tape the comb across the hole. Hold the card at right angles to the table on the white paper.

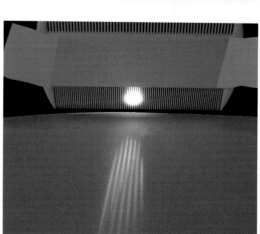

3 In a darkened room, shine the torch through the hole, across the paper.

4 Remove the tape. See the effect of holding the comb at different distances from the hole.

Experiment 2

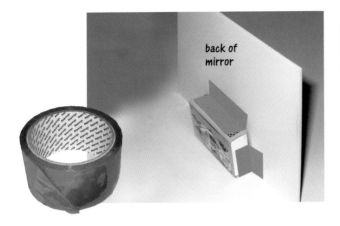

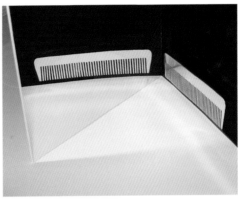

1 Tape the plastic mirror to the empty matchbox so that it will stand at right angles to the table.

2 Set up the mirror on the left. Place the card and a bigger comb on the right, with the torch behind the card.

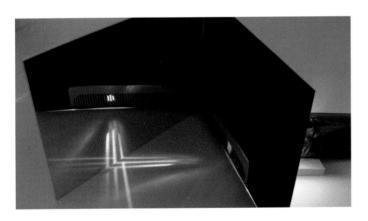

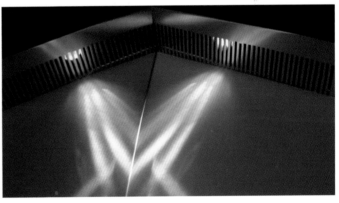

3 In a darkened room, switch on the torch. The rays are interrupted by the mirror. What do you notice about the angles that the light makes with the mirror?

4 Try moving the mirror to lots of different angles.

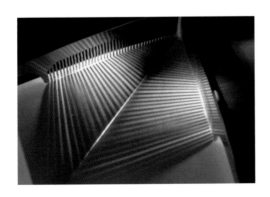

5 Let light creep under the card.

What's going on?

The light hits the mirror at an angle and is always reflected at the same angle.

Jargon Buster

The **angle of incidence** is the angle between the direction of light falling on a surface, and the *perpendicular* from the surface.

Refraction

When light travels from one *medium* to another, for example, from air to glass or from air to water, it changes direction. This is called *refraction*. It's how lenses work!

The plan

We are going to show how refraction occurs and then make a small lens from water.

25 minutes

You will need:

- a friend to help you
- mug (or straight-sided container you can't see through)
- jug of water
- card
- clear sticky tape
- plastic dropper
- button

Experiment 1

1 Put the button in the empty mug.

2 Move the mug away from you until the button is just out of sight.

3 Keep your eyes in exactly the same place and ask your assistant to pour water slowly into the mug. The button reappears!

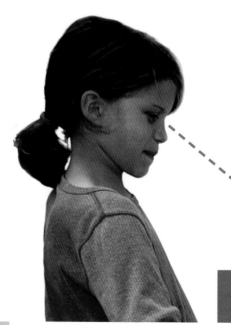

What's going on?

Light changes direction as it passes from the water into the air, so the path of the light coming from the button is 'bent'.

Experiment 2

1 Take a small piece of card and punch a hole in it.

2 Cover the hole with clear tape. Rub over the tape to stretch and indent it slightly.

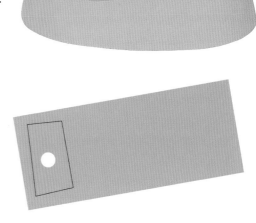

3 Use the plastic dropper to place a drop of water on the plastic tape over the hole.

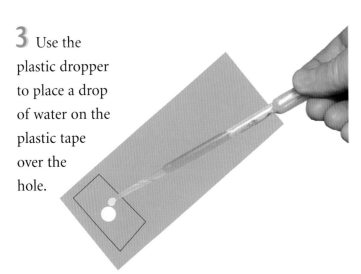

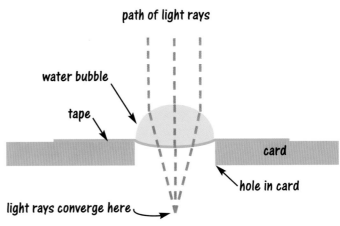

path of light rays

water bubble

tape

card

hole in card

light rays converge here

What's going on?

Light is bent at the curved surfaces, between the water and the air. The lower surface of the water follows the shape of the tape; the upper surface is a natural curve created by surface tension. The curves bend light by slightly different amounts across their surfaces.

What else can you do?

Make the biggest lens you can by this method. Does it magnify any more than the smallest one you made? What do you think limits the size?

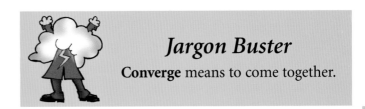

Jargon Buster
Converge means to come together.

Spectrum

Have you ever wondered how a rainbow is formed?
Daylight, or 'white light', is actually made up of lots of different colours mixed together, called the visible spectrum. A rainbow is formed when white light passes through droplets of water in the air.

You will need:

- large bowl, scissors
- water, clear plastic bottles
- plastic mirror, marker pen
- coloured plastic or sweet wrapper
- white card, string, coloured papers, paints, old ballpoint pen

The plan

We are going to make a spectrum from white light and a spinner you can make from card and string!

Experiment 1

1 On a sunny day, take the bowl outside and fill it with water.

2 Put the mirror into the water and *reflect* sunlight up and onto the white card. Move the mirror around until you find the best angle.

3 The reflected light should look something like this.

Jargon Buster

Remember the colours of the spectrum by learning this saying:
Richard of York gave battle in vain –
red, orange, yellow, green, blue, indigo, violet

What's going on?

Light passes from air to water, strikes the mirror and passes back out to the air again. Light is refracted each time it goes between different materials. The colours that make up white light are each refracted at slightly different angles. The result is the spectrum – red, orange, yellow, green, blue, indigo and violet. The last two are usually much fainter than the others and quite hard to see.

What else can you do?

Use a sheet of coloured plastic or sweet wrapper and hold it between the Sun and the water. What happens to the refracted light?

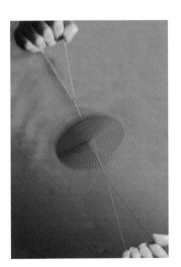

Experiment 2

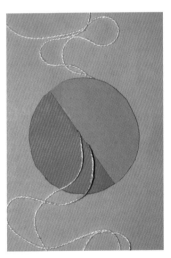

1 Draw round a lid on a piece of stout white card. Now cut out the disc with scissors.

2 Make two holes in the middle with a ball-point pen. Thread the string through and tie the ends.

3 Paint green and red on one side, or stick on two pieces of coloured paper.

4 Now spin the spinner! When the strings twist, pull gently. What colours can you see?

What's going on?

Your eye cannot react fast enough to each colour in turn so you see a blend of the two colours. Red and green together should produce a warm grey.

What else can you do?

Try painting the disc with different colours. What new colours can you see?

Pepper's ghost

45 minutes

Here's an experiment that's part science and part magic trick, and all about not necessarily believing what we see. It gets its name from 'Professor' John Pepper, the 19th century scientist who *perfected* this effect.

You will need:

- cardboard box – about 300 x 225 x 375 mm (12 x 9 x 15 in), tape
- sheets of stout black paper
- clear plastic – same size as one face of box
- night light with holder, matches
- postal tube – about 75 mm (3 in) diameter, 150 mm (6 in) tall, sheet of card
- glass of water, glue stick, paints, brushes

The plan

We are going to reveal the secret of Pepper's ghost.

What to do:

1 Measure 25 mm (1 in) in from the edges of one side of the box and cut a window.

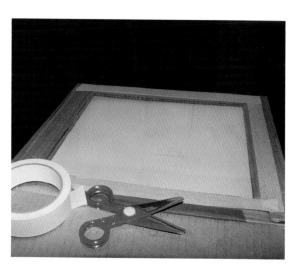

2 Using the glue and tape, line the inside of the box with black paper, except for the window. Fix the plastic over the window with tape.

3 Ask an adult to help you cut a piece out of the postal tube, about a quarter of its *circumference*, from top to base. Line the inside of the rest of the tube with black paper.

14

4 Light the night light and place it in front of the box. Fill the glass with water. Find the position of the *virtual* image of the night light and put the glass inside the box.

5 Position the tube so that the candle is totally screened from the front.

6 Now view the effect from the front. The candle should seem to be still burning underwater!

What's going on?

Normally we can see straight through clear plastic and in daylight it appears as if all the light goes through. In fact, a small amount is reflected, but in daylight it's too faint to see.

In our experiment, we've constructed a special arrangement where all you see is lit by the candle. We've placed the glass exactly so that the candle's virtual image (its reflection in the plastic) is in the same place.

What else can you do?

Use your box to make more 'magical' effects. Create a 19th century Victorian theatre by copying this one onto thin card. Fix the decorated card to the front of the box. Put cut out photographs of friends in place of the candle, and photographs from magazines of unusual places in the box. You'll need two small torches, to make it work. Good Luck! Gather an audience to watch your show!

'Fibre optics'

You will need:

- glass or glass container
- water, a little milk
- plastic bottle with a screw top
- kitchen foil, kitchen sink
- torch, water, tape
- small screwdriver
- a friend to help you
- kitchen you can make dark

Modern telecommunications systems use
light to carry information instead of electricity.
How does light travel along bendy glass cables (fibre
optics) if light can only go in straight lines?

The plan

We are going to show
how fibre optics work.

Ask friends to help.

Experiment 1

1 Fill a glass container with
water. Add a few drops of milk.

2 Put some kitchen foil round
the end of your torch and make a
slit in it.

3 Darken the room. With the slit horizontal, shine the torch up
through the side of the glass, adjusting the angle until light reflects down
from the surface of the water.

Experiment 2

1 Cover the bottle with foil, using tape to hold it in place. Leave the base of the bottle uncovered.

2 Make a hole in the side of the bottle near the top.

3 Cover the hole with your thumb and fill the bottle with water.

4 Replace the screw top. Keep your thumb over the hole. Turn the bottle upside down. Hold the lit torch against the base.

5 Get your friend to turn off the lights. Remove your thumb from the hole. The water escaping should pick up light from the torch.

What's going on?

In Experiment 1, when the angle between the surface of the water and the light beam is great enough, light is reflected back.

In Experiment 2, because of the large angle at which the light hits the boundary between the stream of water and the air, it is reflected back into the water. When it hits the other side of the stream, the same thing happens. This is called total internal reflection. The light only escapes when the water stream hits the sink and scatters.

Mixing colours

We know that when we mix two different colours of paint together we get a third one. The colours we get when we mix coloured light are quite different.

The plan

We are going to compare two ways of mixing colour.

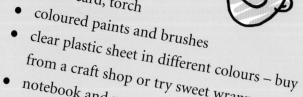

You will need:

- white card, torch
- coloured paints and brushes
- clear plastic sheet in different colours – buy from a craft shop or try sweet wrappers
- notebook and pencil
- darkened room

Experiment 1

1 Mix up three patches of thick colour – blue, red and green.

2 While the paint is wet, use a clean dry brush to blend the edges of the patches together. First blend blue into red.

3 Then clean your brush and blend red into green.

4 Finally blend all three colours together.

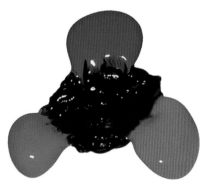

What's going on?

The blends between the three colours are muddy and less bright than the colours that make them.
Paint is made to absorb all the other colours of light and only reflects its own.

Experiment 2

1 This time we're going to use coloured plastic to filter the light from a torch.

2 Work in a darkened room. Shine your torch onto white card. Try the coloured filters one at a time, then try combining two or three. Write down your results.

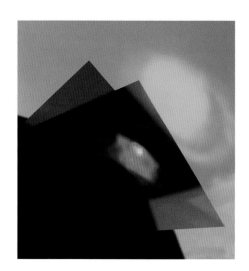

3 Try red and blue. You should see magenta.

4 Blue and green makes cyan (turquoise).

5 Green and red make yellow.

What's going on?

The results are quite different from those produced by using paint. Mixing our red and blue paint produced a dull brownish purple. When we add red and blue light, we get a bright magenta.

What else can you do?

Find combinations of filters that block the light.

Jargon Buster
A filter lets only part of a spectrum go through it.

Sound travel

Sound travels to our ears through the air by making the *molecules* in the air vibrate, but it can also pass through solid materials in the same way.

You will need:

- a friend to help you
- string, metal objects, for example, cutlery, coat hanger
- clean, empty yogurt pots
- hammer and nail

The plan

We are going to show that sound can pass through solid materials.

Find a friend.

Experiment 1

1 Tie the ends of two lengths of string to objects and hold the other ends against your ears.

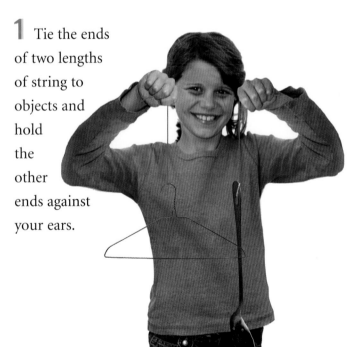

2 Swing the object so that it bangs against something (could be a wall) or get your friend to hit the spoon with something solid. Now try using both objects.

What's going on?

When the object is hit, it vibrates, making a sound which we can hear normally. As we are suspending the objects on taut string, the vibration will travel up the string, making it vibrate. Because we have our fingers pressed into our ears, we can't hear normally through the air, but we can hear the transmitted vibration coming up the string.

Experiment 2

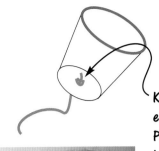

Knot the string inside each yogurt pot. Pull the string tight between the pots.

1 Get your string and two clean yogurt pots ready to make a great telephone.

2 Ask an adult to make a hole in the base of each pot with a hammer and nail, then fix a long piece of string between them.

3 Give the other pot to a friend. Stand some distance apart, keep the string tight, listen or speak!

4 How long can you make the string and still hear the person at the other end?

Experiment 3

Next time you are in a wood, look for a felled tree and get your friend to press his or her ear against one end. Go to the other end and gently gently tap or scratch against the trunk. How small can you make that noise before the other person can't hear you?

'Seeing' sound

25 minutes

Of course we can't actually see sound, but we can see its effect!

The plan

We are going to show that sound travels in waves.

You will need:

- large bowl, cling film
- 2 large empty plastic bottles
- plastic sheet, cut from a carrier bag
- tape, feathers, tissue paper, rice
- container used for savoury snacks
- hammer and nail, scissors, balloon

Experiment 1

1 Stretch some cling film over the top of the bowl. Sprinkle some dry rice grains over the surface of the cling film.

What's going on?

The sound of the plastic bottles banging together *transmits* through the air in waves and causes the cling film to *vibrate*, bouncing the rice up and down.

Jargon Buster
The **decibel (dB)** is the unit used to measure sound level.

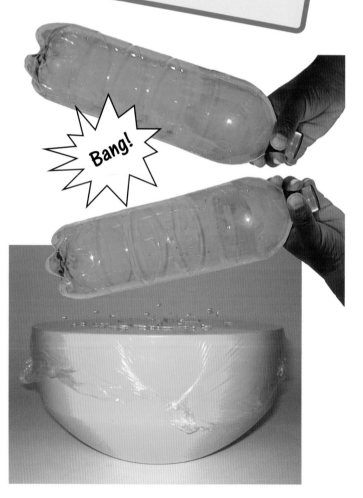
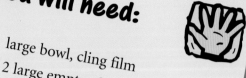
Bang!

2 Bang two plastic bottles together!

Experiment 2

1 Ask an adult to make a hole in the closed end of the container. We used a nail and hammer.

2 Take the piece of carrier bag plastic and stretch it over the open end of the tube. Hold the piece of plastic firmly in place with sticky tape.

3 Point the end with the hole towards the feathers or little bits of tissue paper. Tap the plastic at the other end sharply.

What's going on?

When you hit the plastic, the sound waves pass down the tube and out through the hole, moving the feathers. This is the *shock wave* that causes damage in an explosion.

What else can you do?

Hold an inflated balloon against your ear and ask someone to speak very close to the other side. You can feel the vibrations.

In tune?

Sound is produced in lots of ways. Here's a method of producing different sounds using the same equipment.

You will need:

- several similar glass bottles
- water, food colouring (optional)
- paper and pencil
- stick or ruler

The plan

We are going to see how sounds of differing pitch are produced.

What to do:

1 Fill the bottles with water to different levels. Put the bottles in a line. Put them in order – most water to least water. We've coloured ours, but it's not necessary for the experiment.

2 Test them for pitch by striking each bottle (gently) with a stick. Strike each bottle in the same place.

3 Use the same set of bottles. Now blow across the top of each bottle in turn. Try and get a clear note.

What's going on?

Sound is made by creating vibrations in a material. These vibrations are carried through the air to our ears as waves.

In Step 2, the sound is made by a sharp blow of the stick making the combination of water and glass vibrate. The more water there is in the bottle, the lower the pitch, and the less water, the higher the pitch.

In Step 3, the sound is made by vibrating a volume of air. The greater the volume of air, the lower the pitch, and the smaller the volume of air, the higher – exactly the opposite result to Step 2.

What else can you do?

You could make two sets of bottles to play *duets* with a friend – one set for hitting, one for blowing!

Jargon Buster
Pitch means how high or low a sound is.

Reflection of sound

Sound can be reflected in much the same way as light. It's what happens when you hear an *echo*.

The plan

We are going to find out whether sound follows the same rules as light when it is reflected.

You will need:

- a friend to help you
- 2 cardboard tubes (from kitchen foil or similar), notebook, pencil
- stiff card, shoe box, scissors
- sticky tape, ticking clock

What to do:

1 Cut a round hole in the side of the box and fit a tube to it.

2 Put the box and tube on a table. Place the sound source (the clock) inside the box.

3 Put the other tube on the table with one end near the open end of the first tube.

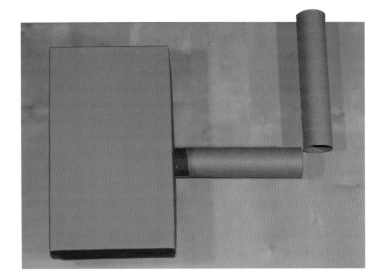

4 Put your ear to the end of the tube and get your assistant to hold a piece of cardboard where the ends of the tubes meet. Note the position of the card when you can hear the clock best.

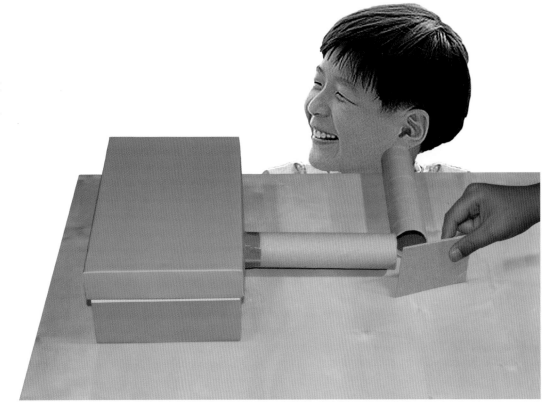

What's going on?

The sound is funnelled down the first tube and reflected by the card into the second tube, but only if the angle between the card and both tubes is the same – just like light.

What else can you do?

Try using different materials instead of the card to see if some things reflect better than others.

Seeing round corners

The *periscope* is a device that uses mirrors to let us see round things. It's a good way to see over the heads of crowds!

25 minutes

You will need:

- empty carton – clean, dry fruit juice carton or similar-size box
- 2 plastic mirrors – each about 75 x 50 mm (3 x 2 in)
- ruler, scissors, parcel tape, marker pen

The plan

We're going to make a simple periscope.

What to do:

1 Remove any plastic spout and seal the box with tape. Measure the depth of the box (**D**) and mark the same distance up the side.

2 Measure the diagonal (**X**). Using the ruler, draw the outline of a square flap on the bottom of the front of the box (black line). Take care to use the same measurement (**X**) for the height and width of the flap.

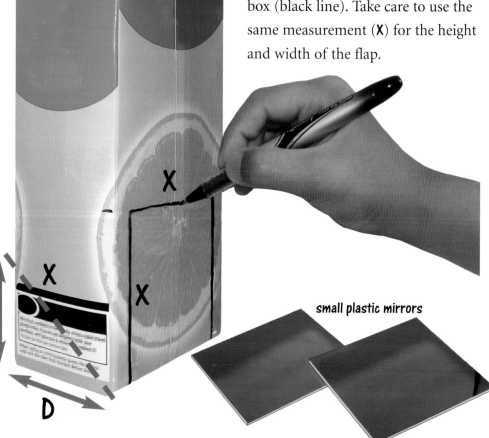

small plastic mirrors

3 Carefully cut three sides of the flap and fold inwards. Use sticky tape to fix the flap at a 45° slant.

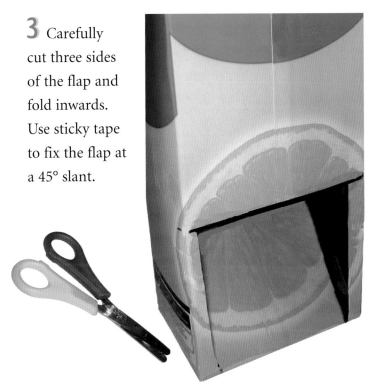

4 Cut a flap at the top of the box on the other side, the same size (**X** by **X**) as before. Fix this flap, again at a 45° slant, with tape.

5 Stick one mirror to each flap with some universal glue.

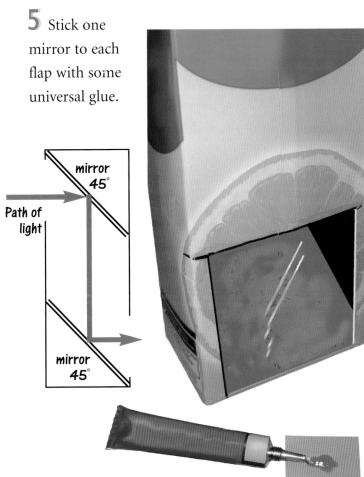

6 Now test your periscope!

See next page for how to decorate your periscope!

What's going on?

Light travels in straight lines.
The first mirror changes the direction of the light by reflecting it, then the second mirror changes it back, parallel to its original path.

25 minutes

Get all your friends together.

What else can you do:

Make sure everyone makes his or her periscope following pages 28–29. Use coloured paper to cover your boxes, and fix with glue sticks. Don't cover either of the viewing windows! Otherwise just go mad with paint and stickers!

Take your periscopes to sports events, you will be able to see over other spectator's heads! When they are decorated you can keep your periscopes as favourite toys.

Glossary

Circumference	The enclosing boundary of a circle.
Convert	To change something in form, character or function.
Duet	Music for two players.
Echo	A sound caused by the reflection of sound waves from a surface back to the listener.
Essential	Absolutely necessary, extremely important.
Illusion	An unreal image or impression, a false idea.
Lens	A piece of glass with one or both sides curved for concentrating or dispersing light rays.
Medium	A substance through which sensory impressions or physical forces can travel.
Molecules	Groups of atoms bonded together making the smallest units of a compound.
Perfected	Made perfect, having completed a project to perfection.
Periscope	A tube or box containing mirrors, designed to increase vision in submarines.
Perpendicular	Upright, at 90 degrees to the horizontal.
Precise	Exact, accurate in every detail.
Predictable	Always behaving in a way that is expected.
Reflect	To throw back light, heat or sound.
Refraction	(of water, air or glass) Making a ray of light change direction.
Shock wave	An intense travelling pressure wave caused by explosion or body of air moving faster than sound.
Telecommunications	A branch of technology relating to sending messages over a distance by cable, telegraph, telephone or broadcasting.
Transparent	Allowing light to pass through so that objects behind can be clearly seen.
Transmit	To pass from one place or person to another. To send a message or an electrical signal, radio or television programme to a receiver.
Vibrate	To move with small movements rapidly side to side or up and down.
Virtual	Not really existing as a solid object, appearing as an image or reflection.

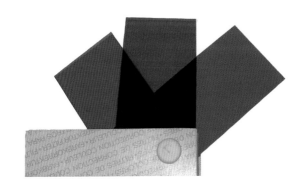

Index

Websites

http://kids.nationalgeographic.com/Activities/FunScience

http://pbskids.org/zoom/activities/sci/

http://sciencemadesimple.com/

http://www.sciencekidsathome.com/